Original title:
"Buddha's Path to Enlightenment"
Copyright © 2023 Loomevalgus OÜ
All rights reserved.
ISBN 978-9916-9874-3-8

You, yourself,
as much as anybody in the entire universe,
deserve your love and affection.

Holding on to anger is like grasping a hot coal with the intent of throwing it at someone else; you are the one who gets burned.

We live in illusion and the appearance of things. There is a reality. We are that reality. When you understand this, you see that you are nothing, and being nothing, you are everything. That is all.

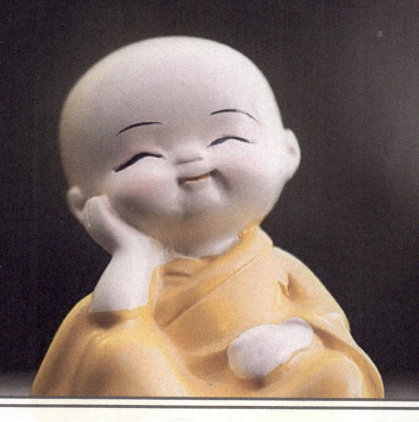

PEACE IS THE HIGHEST BLISS

Do not dwell in the past, do not dream of the future, concentrate the mind on the present moment.

However many holy words you read, however many you speak, what good will they do you if you do not act on upon them?

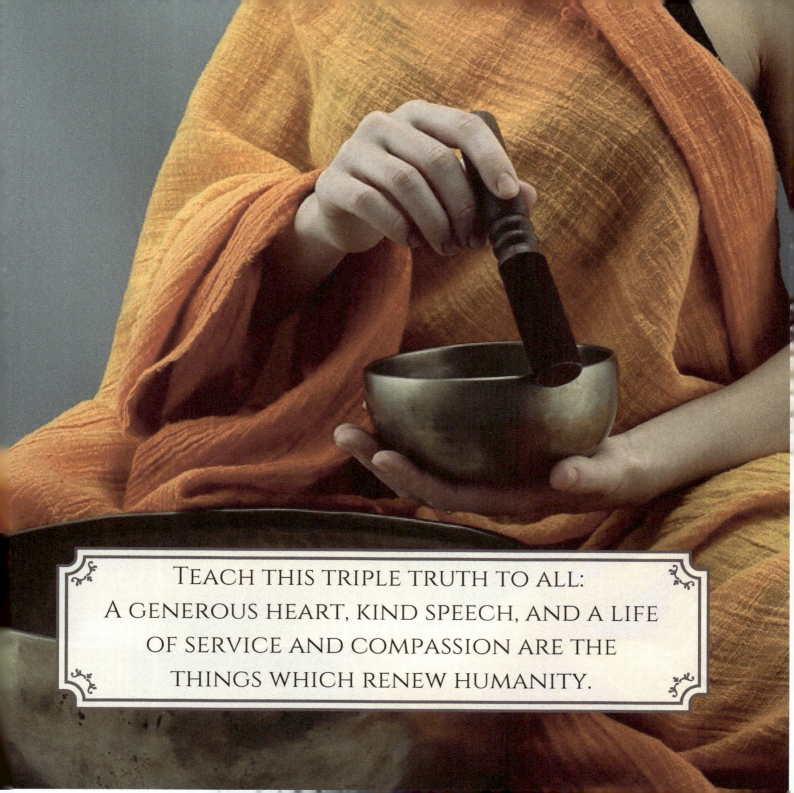

TEACH THIS TRIPLE TRUTH TO ALL: A GENEROUS HEART, KIND SPEECH, AND A LIFE OF SERVICE AND COMPASSION ARE THE THINGS WHICH RENEW HUMANITY.

You should respect each other and refrain from disputes; you should not, like water and oil, repel each other, but should, like milk and water, mingle together.

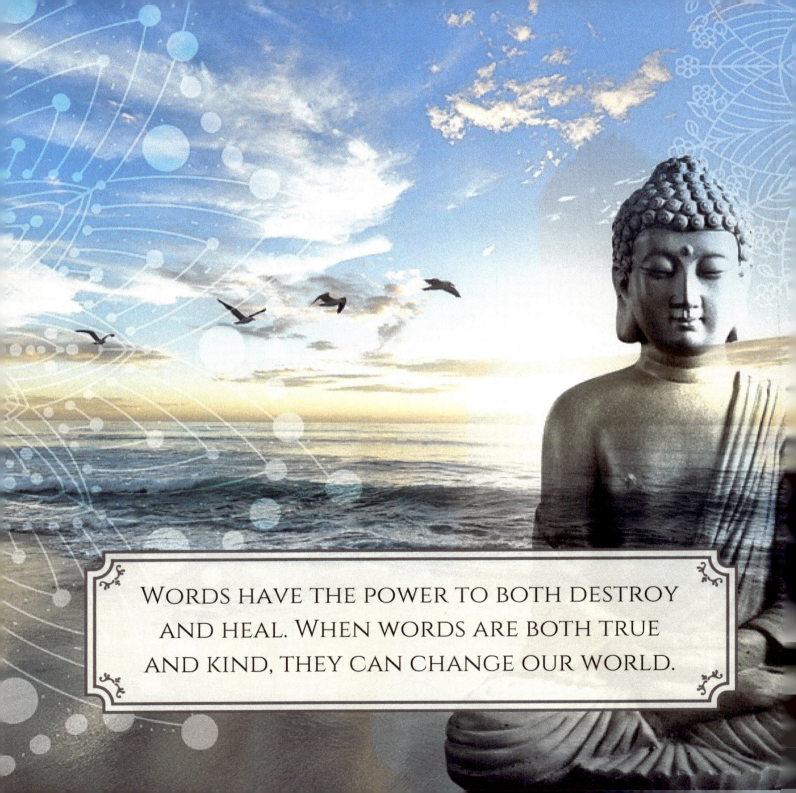

A GOOD FRIEND WHO POINTS OUT MISTAKES AND IMPERFECTIONS AND REBUKES EVIL IS TO BE RESPECTED AS IF HE REVEALS A SECRET OF HIDDEN TREASURE.

Health is the greatest gift, contentment the greatest wealth, faithfulness the best relationship.

CPSIA information can be obtained
at www.ICGtesting.com
Printed in the USA
LVHW072029010323
740706LV00024B/2030